# MORE THAN ORDINARY

## *wisdom:*

### stories of faith and folly

KIT AND DREW COONS

More Than Ordinary Wisdom: Stories of Faith and Folly

© 2018 Kit and Drew Coons

ISBN: 978-0-9995689-5-8

All rights reserved. No part of this publication may be reproduced or transmitted in any form or by any means, electronic, mechanical, including photocopy, recording, or any information storage and retrieval system, without permission from the publisher. Requests for permission to make copies of any part of this publication should be sent to: https://morethanordinarylives.com/

Unless otherwise noted, all Scripture quotations are taken from the New American Standard Bible (NASB). Copyright © 1960, 1962, 1963, 1968, 1971, 1972, 1973, 1975, 1977, 1995 by The Lockman Foundation

Edited by Jayna Richardson
Design: Julie Sullivan (MerakiLifeDesigns.com)

First Edition

Printed in the United States

22 21 20 19 18    1 2 3 4 5

# contents

Why Stories?........................................1

God + Homework = A Miracle....................3

Eat Your Fish and Have it too...................5

Christmas Hope...................................9

African Angel....................................13

When I Shot my Neighbor......................17

Drug Dealers....................................21

Frogs on the Floor..............................25

Who is Running Your Life?.....................27

Syrian Hospitality...............................31

Safeguards......................................37

Hispanic Good Samaritan......................41

Forgiveness Changes Lives....................43

A Tennis Lesson................................47

Personal Testimony............................51

# WHY *stories?*

My wife, Kit, and I once attended a seminar led by two men and one woman. The men both spoke impressively. The woman didn't. She did nearly everything speakers are taught to avoid. She rambled, lost her place in her own notes, looked at the ceiling, and even talked to herself while speaking. But this lady touched the audience's hearts. How? She told story after story. I can't remember a single thing either man said. But I still remember her stories.

Jesus also told story after story, which we call "parables." Who can forget Jesus' story of the Good Samaritan? This powerful, clear lesson speaks to us from a vastly different culture and across the centuries. The power of stories is why Jesus used so many. Stories can enable us to communicate God's truth in a clear, relevant manner. They inspire hope and change lives by speaking to the heart. Our own personal stories, mistakes made and lessons learned, provide contemporary examples.

"I don't want to talk about myself," some insist. They're in good company. Neither did Apostle Paul. "I am speaking as a fool," he wrote as the Holy Spirit forced him to reveal his experiences. (2 Corinthians 11:21) Later in Acts 26, when Paul gave a message to powerful men, he chose not to expound from his great knowledge. Rather, Paul told his personal story, including persecuting the church. Paul communicated in a humble, engaging manner, which almost persuaded King Agrippa.

But the most important audience for our stories is ourselves. God is continually seeking to teach us through our experiences, just as He did to hundreds of men and women documented in the Scriptures. What can we learn by reviewing our own lives? What can our stories of faith and folly communicate about God to others?

The following collection of personal stories is offered for your amusement and to encourage you to look at your own life experiences. What can God teach you even years later from your own life? Are you willing to share that with others?

*Let the redeemed of the Lord tell their story.*
*(Psalm 107:2 NIV)*

To overlook one's own faults is to miss a valuable free education.[1]

---

1. *The Daily Walk*, (Illinois, Walk Thru the Bible Ministries, Volume 16, Number 2, February 1994)

# GOD + HOMEWORK = *a miracle*

My grades in engineering school were very important to me. They seemed to be my best chance to get a great job after graduation. Maybe the job and grades were too important; I studied nearly all the time.

Then, through a student ministry on campus, I became a follower of Christ and got involved in Christian student activities. I became so involved that I didn't have time to do my homework for an important examination. As the professor passed out the test, I was sick with worry. "God, please save me!" I prayed with all my heart as I opened the exam. To my joy, the questions were just the things I knew. When I got my graded paper back with a high score, I remember thinking, *This is great. Now that I'm a Christian, I won't need to study at all anymore.*

I went back to my Christian activities. When the next examination came up, I wasn't worried. Matthew 21:22

promised, "And all things you ask in prayer, believing, you will receive." I remember praying, "Okay, Lord, I'm believing and asking. You know what to do." Opening that exam, I learned that God is not a genie. He wanted and expected me to do my homework. So it is with wisdom, I believe. Throughout my life God has miraculously bailed me out with a sudden insight on occasion in a critical situation. But for a lifetime of building wisdom, I think He wants us to do our homework.

I know that God wanted me to do well in my studies. But He expected me to do my part—the homework. After I learned to trust God *plus* do my homework, my grades improved dramatically. I graduated with high honor. God used those grades to give me a wonderful job. At only 23, I was a designer of the Space Shuttle. God plus homework resulted in a miracle.

# EAT YOUR FISH AND *have it too*

My sixteenth summer was all about fish. That is, catching fish. While other boys spent their teenage summers earning money or playing baseball, I chased fish. Largemouth bass, bluegills, and catfish filled my dreams awake or asleep. But mostly the dreams were about bass. My fishing tutors—outdoor sports magazines—glorified bass. And I became very good at catching the largemouths. Fish passion had even brought me fame and prizes by my winning the Boy Scout Fishing Jamboree.

Fortunately, my widowed mother owned an isolated cabin on a little river. On school nights, we stayed in town. But the cabin felt like home. Big trees walled the clear and cold river with green. In places, the running water was shallow enough to wade across or catch large crayfish. A mile below the cabin, a 20-foot dam for an old grist mill backed up the river into a serpentine lake. You could still see the big mill stones, which before electricity had ground the local farmers' corn. In a little aluminum boat, I used rod and reel and trot lines to pull a lot of fish from that lake. Nearly every fish is released on today's TV fishing shows. But in those days, when you caught a fish, you ate it. And no fish tastes better than a bass. The white, tender flesh of a young bass simply can't be matched.

Even with the lake, my greatest joy was fishing up the river. Wading stealthily upstream in a pair of old sneakers and cut-off blue jeans did not alert most fish to my coming. Then delicately casting an artificial lure above a ripple, by a log, or in a pocket where fish might wait was a skill I learned through many hours of diligence. For some, the pleasure of practicing that art actually surpasses catching the fish. But not quite for a 16-year-old boy.

Early that spring a strong fish had grabbed my lure by a bed of water plants. To my utter amazement, a beautiful, tawny bronze fish erupted from the water, jumping nearly a yard in the air. It was a smallmouth bass, the most elegant of all fighters according to every outdoor magazine. I'd never seen one so large. The picture of that fish hanging in the air, twisting violently, remains in my mind. And the memory of my lure shaken free and coming back at me remains as well.

Every day all summer I chased that smallmouth bass on the river. Hooked it briefly once or twice. I even resorted to using live crayfish trying to trick that fish. But mostly I just spooked it when I waded near. The smallmouth had learned who I was and what I wanted.

Then the summer was over. And I instinctively knew that was to be my last season of freedom on the river. Fall had passed as well. Even the fish had called it a year. Next year I would be at the university. There I would engage in the serious business of making something of my life, and hopefully not disappoint my family and teachers.

Near dark in the chilly December twilight, I went down to the river bank. Mostly I wanted to feel the rod in my hands and hear the water. These were the last casts in the last days of boyhood. The only spot with enough light remaining to cast was where I had never seen fish before. To my surprise, a big fish grabbed the lure. After a minute of tussle, the smallmouth was in my hands.

Eating it immediately came to my mind. Then a voice in my head said, *Let this one go. For the rest of your life, you can enjoy the thought of this fish and its descendants alive and free in this river.* But, youthful passions being what they are, the thought of tasting its sweet flesh was too much to give up. I killed, cooked, and ate the smallmouth. Before the dishes were cleaned, I felt sorrow. My worthy adversary was gone forever. For a moment of pleasure, I had taken on a lifetime of regret.

One fish is a small price for a teenager to learn such a powerful lesson before leaving home for college and an adventurous life. The wisdom to make careful decisions is worth any fish. That fish helped to make me who I am. For those reasons, I no longer regret eating the smallmouth. Still, it would be wonderful to think of the smallmouth's descendants living in the river. I'm a much older man now. My fingers fumble with fishermen's knots. My eyes squint to bait a hook. Keeping balanced on the slippery river rocks would be impossible. Yet my heart will always have that summer on the river. I've caught many other fish in my lifetime. Most of them, I've let go.

# CHRISTMAS *hope*

I spent most of my childhood in the tropical state of Florida. My brother, sister, and I had never seen snow. We knew all about snow, though. Literature for kids is full of stories involving snow, including enticing pictures. Delicate ice crystals falling from the sky? Snowball fights? Snowmen? Sledding down hills? Snow cream? It all sounded magical to Florida kids. And somehow snow is linked to the perfect Christmas. Even adult stories and movies imply that Christmas just isn't complete without snow.

But neither snow nor Christmas was on our minds in the late summer of 1961. My mother, brother, sister, and I waited for my father to come home from an errand. He would take the whole family bowling that evening. Maybe as a ten-year-old, I could make my first spare. But my father didn't come. To our surprise, a police car stopped in front of the house. The deputy walked slowly to our front door. He told us that my father had been killed in an automobile accident.

Within an instant, my world simply stopped. There would be no more fishing trips. No more playing catch in the yard. No more goodnight kisses. What reason was there to continue living? Within a few days we moved away from all we knew to my mother's home state, Alabama. Everything there seemed different. People talked funny. The other kids played games that I didn't understand. Life wasn't death for me, but it didn't quite seem like living either.

Eventually, a joyless Christmas approached. The season just wasn't the same without my father. And I couldn't even imagine what Christmas Day would be like. All of our family traditions involved him.

In the late afternoon of Christmas Eve, a cold north wind started to blow. The sky clouded over. And a few beautiful snowflakes started to come down—very unusual for Alabama. No weather report had predicted snow. Even the old timers were surprised. During the evening, the snowfall intensified. Who cared about presents or Santa coming? My brother, sister, and I spent every minute watching the snow from the windows. On Christmas morning, six inches of crystal cold purity covered the world outside. And to my eternal joy and amazement, there under the Christmas tree a brand-new sled waited, the first one I had ever seen. It was a miracle! Either that, or Santa got really lucky.

On Christmas Day, we played outside doing all the things with snow that we had heard about until we were nearly frozen. Then I got the strangest new feeling. Life was still worth living. Somebody—that Somebody who was able to make snow— would look out for me. The strange feeling was hope. Before my father died, I'd never needed any hope. Now hope said, "Everything will be alright."

Hope is an essential element of a Christian's life. 1 Corinthians 13:13 lists hope along with faith and love. Have you ever seen a young father and mother who weren't full of hope as they cradled their new baby? Probably not. At Christmas, all of us have a new baby: the baby Jesus. That baby is God's gift of hope for all of us, the essence of Christmas. Jesus' hope says, "Everything will be alright."

# AFRICAN *angel*

As a young man, I chose Deuteronomy 10:20-21 as my lifetime theme scripture. "You shall fear the Lord your God; you shall serve Him and cling to Him, and you shall swear by His name. He is your praise and He is your God, who has done these great and awesome things for you which your eyes have seen." This verse was a choice by faith. I hadn't personally seen any "great and awesome things."

Seeking to serve God, I joined a Christian missionary organization and was sent to Africa as a water engineer working for a Muslim government. That government provided me with a rough cinderblock house near a moderately sized village. Blood from midnight sacrifices of chickens and goats to traditional gods marked rocks on the hill behind the village.

The largest structure in this village was a Christian church made of dried mud-blocks. Tree branches supported a corrugated metal roof. The congregation couldn't afford glass for windows, so big openings in the walls provided light and air.

Mud benches with a veneer of concrete on the top to keep your clothes clean when you sat served as pews. A three-foot hunk of an abandoned train rail hung from a tree outside. The church elders would hit the rail with a hammer to call the people to worship.

Most Sundays, I attended services there, usually three hours long. Men and boys sat on the left side; women, girls, and babies on the right. The women and girls all wore flowing, colorful "wrappers," dresses made from a single unsown piece of cloth. The "wrapper" also served as a baby swaddle. Dozens of babies rested contentedly, pressed against their mother's back. The female side was constantly in motion readjusting babies. Their babies almost never fussed or cried.

Services were always joyful. Guitars and drums accompanied soulful, rhythmic hymns. Sometimes people danced in the aisles. The church made me feel like an honored guest with a seat among the elders. Normally about two hundred worshipers occupied half of the pews. Crowd size was easy to estimate because most Africans, lacking the American requirement for personal space, would sit shoulder to shoulder in the front, even if the back rows remained empty.

I had promised the church elders if electricity ever came to the village, I'd get a projector for a movie. And, eventually, the government's power company brought electricity to our village. This was a time of great joy for the entire community. Late into the night, drums beat and people danced. Early the next day, the elders showed up at my door. They reminded me about my promise of the movie. And I remembered my promise.

So I arranged for a projector—the old type with the film reels, a light bulb, and the whirring sound. Meanwhile the church members fanned out across the countryside asking everybody to come to the church to see a movie about Jesus. Because local churches generally opposed attendance at theaters, which showed movies of sex and violence, this would be the first film most locals had ever seen.

On the afternoon of the movie, I had the projector ready. Before night came, the church was jam-packed. I believe we had five hundred inside that little church. There was simply no more room. And nothing but faces filled the wall openings as latecomers climbed on each other to see. Everyone eagerly waited as darkness deepened. Then the power went out, a common occurrence in this part of Africa. No electricity meant no movie. But no one was giving up his or her place.

I noticed that part of the village still had power. One of the three utility wires leading to the village still carried current. I traced out the lines and stood at the foot of the power pole in despair. *If we just had that wire over there,* I thought, *we could get power to the church.* Then a man I had never seen before appeared at my elbow. He had a pair of insulated pliers in his hand. "I can switch the wires," he offered.

I remember looking back up the pole and thinking, *If the shock doesn't kill him, the fall will for certain.* Next I thought, *I'll do it myself.* But still recovering from malaria, I didn't have the strength to climb the smooth pole, much less switch the wires. Then I looked back at the church and the waiting crowd. Souls were at stake. Jeopardizing this man's life was the hardest decision I ever had to make. "Go ahead and try," I told him.

*15*

Then I watched him inch up the pole like a caterpillar, grip it with his knees, and switch the live un-fused 240-volt power wire. Immediately I ran to the church without even thinking to thank him.

We had electricity to the projector! The movie started! Almost nobody there understood the process of movie making. The Africans thought that they were seeing the actual Jesus caught on film. And they loved him. How could you not? They went crazy at the Resurrection like a sports crowd cheering for a winning touchdown. One of my young disciples gave a message calling for a commitment to Christ. I don't know how many received Christ that night, but more than two hundred adults went through follow-up afterwards. And after that, services at our church had no empty seats.

I never saw the man who switched the wires again. Afterwards I wondered, *What happened? Who was that? Was that an angel?* If not, he almost certainly would have approached me afterwards. And how many people come to church with a pair of insulated pliers? Whether he was an angel or not, I saw a "great and awesome thing" with my own eyes.

Sometimes I've also asked myself, *Why did we need such a dramatic miracle? God could simply have kept the power on.* I have come to realize that the situation may have been a gift just for me. For the rest of my life, whenever my faith might waver, I've remembered my theme scripture and what I saw with my own eyes. The memory of my angel climbing the pole in that moment of crisis has enriched my entire life.

# WHEN I SHOT MY
# *neighbor*

Do you remember your biggest ever surprise? Mine came on a pre-dawn Christmas morning not long after my eighth birthday. Under the Christmas tree I found a brand new 20-gauge shotgun. You might be thinking, *That is a surprise*. Some may shudder at the thought of giving a real gun to an eight-year-old. My father, however, had a plan. As a gun enthusiast himself, he wanted to teach his oldest son responsibility.

That afternoon he took me into the country to try out my new shotgun. But no paper target or old can would suffice for us. Instead, Dad started flinging a round, flat target called a clay pigeon into the air. In flight, the clay pigeon looked like a thin, black line. The target flew away from us so fast that if I blinked, it was gone. At barely eight years old and small for my age, I could hardly hold the gun up. The best I could manage was trying to cover the clay pigeon with the muzzle of the gun and pulling the trigger. After each shot the shotgun's recoil hurt terribly, worse than any spanking. I didn't know much about shooting. I did know instinctively that a man wouldn't acknowledge any amount of recoil pain. And so neither did I.

Eventually I managed to clip a couple of the targets and even smashed one. Dad shouted out with pride in his son. Then my father gave me an unexpected instruction. "I want you to shoot that tree." And he indicated a little pine tree about the size of a baseball bat handle.

"Shoot the tree?" I asked.

"Yes, shoot the tree," he repeated.

Now this still target was more to my liking. No way that this pine tree could fly away. Carefully taking aim and firing, I hit the little pine squarely at my eye level. The damage to the tree shocked me. All the bark had been torn away and the strong wood riddled. "Now, what do you think would happen if you accidentally shot a man?" my father asked. No answer was necessary. I fully understood the gun safety lesson.

A couple of weeks later our whole family had gone on an outing in the country. My dad pointed into a little gully. "I'll bet there are some quail in there," he predicted. Then he pulled my shotgun out of the car trunk and handed it to me along with a couple of shotgun shells. My mother, little brother, and sister could watch me get my first birds. Dad pointed to the right. "I'll go around here. The birds will flush out that way," he explained, waving to the left. "You know what to do."

And I did know what to do. There I stood, an eight-year-old with his finger on the trigger of a loaded gun. With the others watching, I couldn't let those birds escape. My father started around the gully and the birds flew up, but not as he had expected. The birds flew directly between my father and me. Rather than fire, I calmly watched the quail fly away with the gun pointed safely skyward. The safety lesson of the pine tree had saved my father's life. As he came walking back, my mother felt understandably shaken.

She screamed, "I thought you were dead! He could have shot you!"

"It's just a good thing he didn't," Dad answered with gruff pride in his son. That day I felt like a man for the very first time.

Nearly thirty years later, my wife and I lived at the edge of a subdivision with large overgrown fields behind us. On a beautiful crisp fall afternoon, I was enjoying a walk around the backyard. To my surprise a covey of wild quail flew over my head and spread out in the fields. I got my shotgun and went to find the hiding birds. The man who owned the fields was a friend from my church. His son, a young man of 22, heard me shooting at the quail. He brought his shotgun and joined me. As we walked and talked, some quail flew up back toward the subdivision. Without thinking, I fired at them. Immediately, I knew that I had made a mistake. *Nobody will ever know*, I thought.

We continued hunting a while longer, but saw no more birds. I invited him back to my house. To our surprise, my young friend's wife was waiting there in our kitchen with my wife. "You guys stay inside!" she pleaded. "Somebody in the neighborhood has been shot. The police are looking for who did it."

Looking out the front window, I saw a sheriff's patrol car cruising slowly down our street, trying to get a bearing on the shooting. Overcome by guilt, I threw open the front door and ran to catch the police car. Grabbing the door handle, I confessed, "It was me! I shot toward the houses!"

The patrol car stopped, the door opened, and a huge deputy emerged. He was an African American man big enough to wring my skinny neck on the spot. At that moment, a neck wringing would have come as a relief. But he stood there with his hands on his hips just looking at me. "Son, you are a grown man. You should know better than to be so careless. Now, you go tell that lady that you're sorry." And he pointed to the house of our best friends.

Apparently, a few of the shotgun pellets had struck our friend Sherri. Fortunately, those pellets had been spent and hadn't penetrated her skin. The deputy didn't have to force me. Being truly repentant, I approached her, confessed, and asked for forgiveness. When Sherri saw who had shot her, she said, "If it had been anybody but you, I would give them a piece of my mind." Then she proceeded to give me *all* of her mind. She was understandably more upset because her baby had also been outside and could just as easily have been hit. I deserved every bit of her ire. I stayed silently nodding as long as she had anything to say. Her tirade seemed to last forever, but probably was only twenty minutes. After releasing her emotions, Sherri did fully forgive me and sent me home. Our friendship was unaffected.

As I walked home in shame and relief, I realized, *You did better handling a gun when you were an eight-year-old boy.* To this day, I am extremely cautious using firearms and have taught many boys and girls to be the same.

Plus, I learned a deeper lesson. Sometimes we learn the right thing to do from a young age, but when we are grown, we seem to forget or get careless. Perhaps overconfidence is a danger that comes with being an adult. To truly be men, we frequently just need to remember to do what we know is right, and what our fathers taught us.

# DRUG *dealers*

"The police are going to find your bodies in a vacant lot!" the tough guys promised as they encircled us. Nobody likes to hear words like these, especially two young white guys living in an ethnic inner-city neighborhood.

In a few months, I would move to Africa for two years. A Christian missionary organization was sending me into a Muslim area of Nigeria where new missionaries weren't welcome. But water engineers, such as myself, were welcome regardless of their religion.

As part of my missionary training, I had the opportunity to live with an African American host family for three months. A mixture of African Americans and Hispanics populated that inner-city neighborhood. Part of our training was to meet people and talk to them about Jesus. If we couldn't do that effectively in America, we probably couldn't overseas either. Ninety-nine percent of the people living there were law-abiding and friendly. They welcomed us warmly and generously.

However, within that neighborhood lived a few troublemakers, mostly unemployed young men, who made life difficult for everyone. Drug dealing, thievery, and gang-related violence were common. Gunfire disrupted every night, frequently on our street. Filled with fervor for the Lord, my partner and I agreed to spend our afternoons in the neighborhoods seeking out the roughest guys around. "They need Jesus the most," we reasoned. We started asking people we met where to find them.

Now think of this from the perspective of those young men. A couple of preppy white guys were looking for them and asking questions. Naturally they felt suspicious and thought we might be working for the police. As if the police wouldn't know better than to send out anybody so naively obvious.

One afternoon a couple of these guys approached us. "Come back here. We want to show you something." We went blithely along. Out of sight behind a house, a group of them waited for us. They started cursing and pushing us around saying that we were "narks." In the end, I think our dumbness saved us. Even these tough guys realized that the police were too smart to use anyone like us. But they left us with the promise involving our bodies and the vacant lot as a clear warning to stay out of their neighborhood. And they truly meant it!

Did we go back? Of course we did! This was a challenge to our faith. We never hesitated. After all, we would soon be missionaries. We quoted 2 Timothy 1:7, "For God has not given us a spirit of timidity, but of power and love and discipline."

Over several weeks, a few of these young men came to trust us. They became confident enough to sell drugs in front of us. One of them taught me how to hotwire a car. This came in handy later in Africa when my ignition switch failed. Another had a cousin who was an aspiring lightweight boxer. He let me exercise with him. In this case, I knew better than to ever get into the ring with him. Eventually, we led several of these men to Christ. One man demonstrated change by getting his GED and finding a job.

We had felt great risk in going back to those men and also tremendous exhilaration putting our lives on the line for our Lord. This act of spiritual bravado led my partner and me to consider ourselves heroes of the faith.

But eventually I learned that God had used this experience to prepare me for a greater lesson. A year later I lived in Africa and had been sick for months with strep throat, malaria, and dysentery. At night, I cowered under bed covers while rats roamed my room. My fellow missionaries, under stress themselves, couldn't get along. Whereas I had once been willing to be heroic for God, by then all I wanted to do was go home. Jesus wasn't so important to me anymore.

Remembering my previous feeling of heroism, I asked myself, *What happened to me?* Peter's story came to mind. John 18:10 records, "Simon Peter then, having a sword, drew it and struck the high priest's slave, and cut off his right ear." During Jesus' arrest, Peter was ready to fight and die if necessary. Yet before that same night was over, he would three times deny even knowing Jesus. Peter was ready to be a hero. He wasn't ready to stand firm in difficulty and confusion.

Reading through the Bible, especially the Old Testament, we see many acts of faith and courage. God wants us to live for Him every day, of course. But most of the men and women recorded in Scripture had a special moment of faith and courage as the defining act of their lives. So it is with us. When we get those rare opportunities, we should embrace them. This doesn't necessarily entail bodily risk. Neither does God demand that we prove our faith by taking foolish or reckless chances. "You shall not put the Lord your God to the test." (Luke 4:12)

Being persistent in hardship, especially through illness and confusion, requires more faith and courage than a moment of bravery. Deliberately forgiving when we have been deeply wronged is a heroic act. Loving an enemy, turning the other cheek, and sacrificially giving can all be more heroic than putting our lives at risk.

# FROGS ON THE *floor*

---

As missionaries in the South Pacific, my wife, Kit, and I waited in a rural church in Fiji for a group of students to gather. Our assignment was to talk candidly to them about sex and relationships. When a frog big enough to swallow a mouse hopped down the center aisle, I thought, *This is different.* Then a second frog joined the first, snapping up bugs between the pews. I decided that we needed to remove the frogs before the meeting started. The village children shrieked with laughter at my efforts to chase the frogs between the pews. Finally, with the frogs chased out, we started the meeting.

Fijians love to sing and started with some melodic indigenous songs. Enchanting moments like that are the most enjoyable part of being a missionary. They touched my heart. I wanted to give the people our very best presentation. But during the singing, more huge frogs joined us through the open door. By the time we stood to speak, a dozen tongue-snapping frogs hopped all around our feet. The frogs constantly distracted us while we tried to teach.

Afterwards I fussed to God, "Lord, speaking in another country to a different culture and age group is hard enough without having to worry about stepping on frogs! Why do things have to be so hard?" I demanded in frustration. Immediately God showed me my wrong attitude. I had been more concerned about showing how well I could speak than about the message the Fijians received. They didn't care about the frogs.

As I thought about it, I realized that ministry is nearly always like that. Although we always did the best we could under all circumstances, we almost never had a chance to perform our very best. Our desire to do so could be a reflection of ego. Stress caused by disturbances like a few frogs might be a symptom of wanting to look good rather than serve wholeheartedly. I now know that one reason for the frogs was as a help for me. The difficulty kept me from being consumed by my own ability. I'm reminded of Apostle Paul who was given an affliction for his own good. "Most gladly, therefore, I will rather boast about my weaknesses, so that the power of Christ may dwell in me." (2 Corinthians 12:9)

After our years in the South Pacific, we became part of a global team for a Christian ministry. We have spoken in 39 different countries outside the US, each situation with its own challenges. When the unexpected happens, Kit and I look at each other. Our eyes say, *Frogs on the floor.* I have come to love those frogs as a reminder to not try impressing an audience, but focus on serving the people.

# WHO IS RUNNING *your life?*

---

At barely 23 years old, I became a designer on the Space Shuttle. Major design work had just started at the main orbiter contractor, North American Rockwell, in Downey, California. The same core group of engineers and scientists who had designed the moon landing Apollo program for NASA then worked on the new Space Shuttle. I asked some questions, did some research, and requested a job interview in a key design group.

Young hubris being what it is, getting the job didn't surprise me. My resume would have looked good to NASA: Mechanical Engineering degree with high honor from Auburn, up-to-date computer-aided design skills, and a secret security clearance from the US government. I'd already passed the professional engineering exam, had experience as an engineer on the Delta Rocket program, and had worked as an engineering assistant on the F-15 fighter development. So I could readily read—even produce—aircraft blueprints. But most important, I knew that my relatively low pay would bring the average salary down, thereby increasing Rockwell's profits on the project.

That's how I joined the group of veteran engineering heroes. Those nerdy geniuses with degrees from MIT, Cal Tech, and Stanford, plus years of experience on the Apollo, made even me look cool. My credentials weren't so impressive anymore. I stayed busy keeping the brilliant designers' pencils sharpened and checking their calculations for minor mistakes. I hoped that eventually I'd get my chance. That chance came in a surprising manner.

After a few weeks, the shuttle project director brought in another manager who was more personable, but not as technical, as the manager who had hired me. He instructed the two managers to share the pool of design engineers. That arrangement lasted only a couple of weeks. Their leadership styles were just too different. The project director solved the problem by telling the managers to split the group and the systems to be designed. The original technical manager took all of his brilliant engineers. The new personable manager got me, the old guys, and the paper shufflers. Their primary role, like mine, was to keep the average salary down.

Crushed is not adequate to describe my feelings at being relegated to that group. My dream had been dashed. At the time, I was a new Christian just exploring my faith. I couldn't believe that God would let this happen to me. One of the brilliant engineers, also a Christian and my friend, understood how I felt and came to console me. "Don't you believe that God is running your life?" he gently asked.

"God must be," I answered bitterly. "If I was running my life, I'd be doing a better job!" As the next few days passed, the only reason I didn't resign is that I didn't want the humiliation of going back to my hometown in Alabama defeated.

The personable manager soon realized what had happened. He had been stuck with the workers nobody else wanted. One afternoon he came to my desk, where I sat morosely. He carried an armload of blueprints. "Here, Drew. Just try to do the best you can," he said and dropped the drawings in front of me. Then he simply walked away. I can still remember the tone of hopelessness in his voice.

I've never entered a lottery. But I know the feeling of winning one. I would never have gotten this responsibility while assisting the brilliant engineers. Of course, I first apologized to God. I'm not sure, but it seemed like He laughed at me. For certain, I got an impression of His forgiveness telling me, "It's okay, young one."

Immediately, I started designing our group's portion of the system. The work made me study the advanced chapters in my engineering textbooks, which my professors hadn't been able to cover. And to be honest, the brilliant engineers in the other group coached me a bit privately, especially my Christian friend. Every aspect required fresh thinking for the first reusable spacecraft. Without any Apollo experience, all of my thinking was fresh. I created some significant innovations. Helping to create the shuttle remains a highlight of my life.

Eventually the project director recognized the imbalance of the design groups and brought them back together. Then the brilliant engineers checked my work. My designs all passed with only minor modifications.

Being an Alabama country boy, three years of living in Southern California were enough. I applied and got accepted to graduate school at Georgia Tech. There I specialized in compressible fluid flow, which had been a major area of application working on the shuttle. My thesis in this specialty led to a wonderful job as a research engineer in a small southern town.

The personable manager, who had given me a chance despite misgivings, greatly appreciated my work. He released me from any obligation to return to California, even though Rockwell had paid the tuition for my graduate degree at Georgia Tech.

Proverbs 3:5–6 cautions us, "Trust in the Lord with all your heart, and do not lean on your own understanding. In all your ways acknowledge Him, and He will make your paths straight." Now whenever things in my life haven't worked out as I had planned, I've remembered when I was so arrogant as to think I could run my life better than God. *Take it slow there, fellow,* I tell myself. Sometimes I can sense God still chuckling a bit.

# SYRIAN *hospitality*

"I want your address. I will come to America. I will keel you." The large, surly Arab looked us in the eye as he spoke. As my wife and I glanced at each other, she whispered, "He's kidding, right?" After all, he could kill us right then and there if he really wanted to. *Surely this must be a form of Arabic humor*, we thought. Rather than risk provoking him by refusing and still remain on the safe side, we only gave him our office address.

We traveled through Syria just before the civil war there started. We spoke through a translator to large groups of Christians and some Muslims about having rewarding marriage relationships. We taught in all the places you've seen on the news: Aleppo, Homs, Damascus. About 5% of Syrians are considered Christian—that is, born of Christian parents. Local Christians organized our engagements.

"You are the head of the snake!" another Arab snarled at us regarding America. But not all Syrians felt that way. One young man who served as a tour guide for us expressed admiration for the US. Dressed in jeans and a polo shirt, he studiously acted American and used American lingo. This marked him in Syrian culture as a rebel, a bad boy. Why would he do this? We passed three pretty Muslim teenage girls completely covered by black hijabs except for their faces. Their expressive eyes had been highlighted with heavy false eyelashes and dark liner. To our surprise, the girls took the initiative to call out flirtatiously to the bad boy. He shrugged them off. "Happens all the time," he explained.

Despite a few detractors, most Syrians are hospitable and welcomed us warmly. We generally felt safe when under the protection of our hosts, especially when they housed us in a convent. Hospitality in Syria is equated to personal honor like depicted in the Bible's Old Testament. Many Syrians invited us into their homes where they went to tremendous effort to prepare special Arab dishes for us. One charming Arab custom is that a guest is supposed to adamantly deny food, even if he is starving. The host then insists and, if necessary, takes the guest's plate and piles it with food. Having been in several Arab cultures previously, we knew and followed the customs. This required us to eat and praise everything regardless of any potential consequences.

And consequences there were. After a week, I became as sick as any tourist to Mexico has ever been. Fortunately, we take anti-diarrhea and stomach medicines along on our trips so that we can do our job no matter how badly we feel. But the generous invitations to Arab homes continued to come. Remember the Arab custom about food and hospitality? Regardless of how much I insisted that I couldn't eat, our gracious hosts knew better. I can now testify from personal experience, "I can do all things through Christ who strengthens me."

Every culture also has surprises. Syrians are bird fanciers. Most have in their homes pampered pet birds—parrots, canaries, doves—which are extraordinarily tame and appear to enjoy family festivities. The biggest public activity on Saturdays in Damascus is the "pigeon exchange." Hundreds of men, young and old, gather all morning at an outdoor rendezvous buying, selling, and trading pet birds. Now whenever western media shows Arabs in angry mobs, I also remember the other picture: coarse-looking men gently handling and admiring pigeons.

Our speaking engagements required travel between towns. Buses are the most economical and convenient transport. We had to take one five-hour trip between Aleppo and Damascus without an Arabic-speaking guide. Our hosts bought our tickets and put us on the "luxury express" bus. We enjoyed riding through the barren Syrian desert in cool air-conditioned comfort. About halfway to our destination, the bus stopped in a smaller town. We had been told by our hosts before leaving Aleppo that a stopover of fifteen to twenty minutes would give us a break. I got off the bus to look around and use the toilet.

In my absence, police commandeered the luxury bus and moved it. I came back to find our comfortable bus and my wife had vanished. Nobody could understand my English as I asked where the bus and my wife had gone. Close to panic and watched by hundreds of robed Arabs, I ran everywhere, looking into every bus. Finally, through a thick hedge, I glimpsed a large vehicle moving. After climbing over a ten-foot wrought-iron fence and fighting through the hedge, I found a second bus terminal. There I discovered my wife making quite a spectacle of herself protecting our luggage and trying to keep an alternate bus to Damascus from pulling away and leaving us behind. Someone banged on the side of the bus. The driver stopped just long enough for us to jump on with our suitcases.

This local bus could only be described as decidedly non-luxury, and we had lost our nice seats. In Syria, a woman has the right to not sit next to any man who isn't her husband. Since two seats together no longer remained available, the driver invited my wife to sit in the front next to another woman who traveled alone. I ended up sitting shoulder-to-shoulder on the back bench of the bus with a ragged group of desert dwellers. Their swarthy un-shaven looks would have frightened the mujahedeen's "holy warriors," let alone me. All they needed was bandoleers of bullets across their chests to be picture perfect. Soon, the warm afternoon air and motion of the bus lulled one man next to me to sleep. His turbaned head gradually slipped over onto my shoulder. I "accidentally" kicked his leg, which startled him awake. But gradually his head nodded over onto me again. I sat there thinking, *Not everybody gets a chance to do this.* He woke from his nap as we pulled into Damascus and never seemed to notice his pillow.

Our talks on marriage and relationships in Syria were a sensation. The crowds laughed at our stories and responded with gratitude. Arabs clustered around us after every session expressing personal difficulties with relationships and asking sincere questions. Even the undercover police monitoring us seemed to enjoy our presentations. You can always pick secret police out of an audience because they don't bring a spouse and nobody sits next to them. Serving our fellow man, especially those very different from ourselves, is truly a privilege and an adventure. Adventures are not necessarily fun at the time. And yet, if we embrace them, they will enrich our lives and deepen our understanding of others.

# safeguards

A consultant came to the factory where I worked as an engineer to talk to us about labor relations. Among other things, the consultant emphasized the value of simple courtesy. "Speak to all the hourly employees and smile," he coached. Seems fundamental for most people, but not necessarily for engineers.

The next morning I happened to be a few minutes late to work. As I entered the front gate, the graveyard shift flooded out. *This is a great opportunity*, I figured. *I'll speak to everybody.* And so I tried to make eye contact, speak to, and smile at each person. It didn't work. They walked right by me without noticing, like I was invisible. That is, all but one group. Every attractive young woman spoke to me.

Up in my office I thought, *Wow! All of the young women spoke to me.* Then the meaning hit me like a dead fish in the face. *Those women spoke to you because they expected you to speak to them. You must have spoken to them before.* I hadn't even realized that I had been partial. I immediately changed that behavior. Within a few weeks, nearly all the employees got used to me speaking to them. And if my work required me to talk with a young woman, I deliberately found a reason to go and talk with two older women as well to avoid any appearance of partiality.

Maintaining healthy and appropriate relationships with the opposite sex is serious business, especially in the workplace. Infidelity destroys countless relationships, and Christians are no exception. Even so, few Christian men or women plan to start an unhealthy relationship. It starts more innocently: a compliment, some flirting, a few confidences shared. Moral failure is usually more like the slow leak of a tire rather than a blowout.

As I said, Christians are not exempt. But they are more tempted to find ways to deceive themselves until it is too late. A Christian man who finds himself attracted to another woman, perhaps at work, might share some prayer requests or invite her to a lunchtime Bible study. You're always okay in prayer and Bible study, right? Wrong! Even spiritual involvement can lead to dangerous emotional or physical involvement.

Safeguards are necessary to protect our hearts. My wife, Kit, and I made a special commitment several years ago. We had observed several Christians, including prominent leaders, fail morally. We asked God to do us a favor. We asked God, who can see into our future, to take our lives before we would do anything sexual or otherwise that would cause Him dishonor. Now there's a safeguard for you.

After the commitment, and remembering the incident with the women, I got a little nervous. *You don't want to get too near the edge, Drew,* I reasoned. So I went to the engineers I worked with, including both Christians and non-Christians. I told them candidly about our commitment to God and asked them, "If you see me flirting with a woman or having any involvement that might even lead to trouble, I want you to do me a favor by telling Kit." Now there's an even bigger safeguard. Actually, I'm sort of hoping if the need arises, that God gets to me first. Kit jokes that God would just kill me. In her case, torture would be involved.

The point is that we can't be too careful. Our responsibility is to safeguard our hearts.

# HISPANIC *good samaritan*

---

The area near our home in the Ouachita Mountains of Arkansas is wonderful for cycling. Country roads wind between forest and fields, homes and farms. There are enough hills to make the rides challenging, but not so many severe ones to break your heart. Lots of competitive bike teams and clubs use our area for practice.

Many Hispanics have immigrated to Arkansas, particularly in recent years. I never spoke or acted negatively against any Hispanics. But I didn't know any personally. And sometimes I'd notice these immigrants and think, *There are a lot more of "them" around.*

On a late summer afternoon, I started a forty-mile loop on my road bike beginning and ending at my house. I had just managed to pass a bike team for the first and only time in my life, when *pop*—my rear tire blew. The bike team, which I had gloated over in my heart, stopped to help. But none of us could fix it. "Thanks, guys. I'll hitch a ride home," I said and sent them on.

I remained twenty miles from home with a flat tire and no cell phone. Hitchhiking is not my thing. But I have done so by necessity. And this day I needed to try. You've perhaps heard that people in the country are friendly and helpful. Not this day—at least not for a bicyclist. Nobody would stop. Carrying my bike and in my riding clothes, my need for a ride would have been obvious. I couldn't help but notice all the fancy and empty pickup trucks that passed me by.

Finally, I gave up and started walking the twenty miles back home in the hot sun. *Should make it by nightfall,* I thought. Suddenly there was a *beep, beep* behind me. Turning around, I saw an old pickup truck. A short, dark-complexioned young man wearing a straw cowboy hat sat behind the steering wheel. He smiled and waved me on board. With the bike in the back of the truck and me in the passenger seat, I started trying to talk to my benefactor. To my surprise, he spoke limited English. He could tell me that he had come from Mexico to find work and support a wife and two children back home. He had been in the US for nearly two years.

Turned out that he wasn't going my way, but he changed directions and took me home anyway. After he dropped me off, I couldn't help but think, *Drew, aren't you ashamed? You probably wouldn't have stopped to pick him up.*

Jesus' parable of the Good Samaritan came immediately to my mind. Most Jewish people looked down on the Samaritans, yet the Samaritan stopped to help the injured man when others would not. I'll bet that the victim in Jesus' story never thought about Samaritans in the same way again. And I won't think about immigrants the same way either.

# FORGIVENESS
*changes lives*

---

In the 1980s, a Muslim government controlled Nigeria. They didn't welcome Christian missionaries. Not even America's Peace Corps was welcome. But that Muslim government accepted engineers regardless of their religion. To get missionaries into Nigeria, a Christian organization found a job for me as a water engineer working for the Nigerian government.

I became the maintenance engineer for water supplies in 19 towns. At first, only one station was pumping water. The other 18 had all broken down for lack of maintenance or spare parts. Hundreds of people were dying of cholera, typhoid, and other waterborne diseases.

I started by organizing the mechanics and electricians and setting up a workshop. Gradually the workers and I brought all 19 stations into service. Nigerians came running with buckets and bottles to fill with fresh water. Children shrieked and laughed as if we were giving away candy.

However, a few of the Nigerians felt jealous at my success. One, a man whom I had replaced, went to headquarters and reported some terrible and untrue things about me. At the time, I was sick from malaria and dysentery and still trying my best. How could he make things harder? I found myself hating this man and even hoping he would die. Then I realized, *You are a Christian missionary. How can you justify hating anyone?*

As an act of faith, I deliberately forgave this man. I determined to take no steps to retaliate. Furthermore, I would give him a blessing. "Do not repay evil with evil or insult with insult. On the contrary, repay evil with a blessing." (1 Peter 3:9, NIV) I started to go out of my way to be nice, even speaking well of him in front of other people. God softened his heart, and we began to get along well.

Several other Christians and I organized an outreach. This former adversary attended and committed his life to Christ. Never have I seen God change a man so fast. He left the meeting and stopped each person he met, saying, "I just became a Christian. You can become one, too."

The ability God gave me to forgive made this man's life change possible. Forgiveness is a command from God so Christians can represent Him well, and yet it is also a privilege given to make our lives better. *US News & World Report* magazine conducted research on the subject of happiness. They reported that the single most important factor for whether a person leads a happy life is the ability to forgive others. Somebody once said, "Failing to forgive is like drinking poison and hoping the other person will die."

Admittedly, sometimes when I am hurt, forgiveness seems impossible. When this happens, I first remember Jesus' death for me. Then I consider his Word: "Be kind and compassionate to one another, forgiving each other, just as in Christ God forgave you." (Ephesians 4:32) Then by faith, I make a prayerful decision to forgive that person and not take any steps to punish them. Finally, I deliberately do good for them. I've found that my heart softens as I serve them as a person for whom Christ also died. The ability God gives me to forgive has changed my life.

# A TENNIS *lesson*

---

I played competitive tennis for twenty years. After marriage, my young wife, Kit, took up the game as well. As she started to improve, she had an idea: "We could have fun playing doubles against other couples." Now, that can be a test of anybody's marriage. You know how they have engaged couples go through premarital counseling? I think they should make them play tennis together to learn how their future spouse might respond under pressure.

The problem came because I wanted to win more than anything. People play tennis for fun, right? Well, losing provided no fun for me. Therefore, when we started playing together, I began telling Kit the mistakes she was making on the court. I pointed out lots of ways she ought to improve her game.

To my surprise, she started playing poorly in our matches. As I continued telling her everything she needed to do differently, her play became worse. I felt like every time she could touch the ball with her racket, the other side got a point. Finally in one match I told her, "Serve the ball and step off the court. I'll play them by myself."

But I couldn't win tennis doubles that way. Kit didn't literally leave the court, but she really was out of that match. Our opponents passed me down the sideline. I had to ask Kit to cover the line. She did, and we came from behind to win.

That day I started to discover the power of godly encouragement. The way Kit played tennis was directly related to the way I treated her on the court. Whenever I started to criticize her, she played awful. But when she had fun, when I encouraged her, she played well. It was a living example to me of the power of 1 Thessalonians 5:11: "Therefore, encourage one another and build up one another, just as you also are doing."

This experience was the beginning of God developing in me the ability to encourage others. Encouragement isn't telling a person what you think they should do, a "You can do it!" pep talk, or false praise. Real encouragement begins with discovering and praising what a person does well. Building someone up involves maximizing their strengths. In tennis, Kit's crosscourt forehand was her best shot and more consistent than mine. So we positioned her on the tennis court to take advantage of that shot.

Acknowledgment of strength in one area can even give a person confidence to improve in other areas. Soon Kit's other shots became strong enough that we could switch our positions on the court in the middle of a point. This really confused our opponents. Minimizing inherent weaknesses can also be part of building up one another. For example, Kit's upper body was not strong enough for her to smash a tennis ball over her head. Whenever possible, I would hit those shots.

After I learned these principles, Kit played better and better tennis. She became so good that we played in a tennis league one summer where she was the only woman in the league. All the others were men who, like me, wanted to win. We played for a position on our team and won a starting spot. Together we won over half of our matches and had lots of fun together. I never had so much fun playing tennis as that summer with Kit. I enjoyed losing with Kit more than winning with anybody else. And the fun came because I had learned how to encourage.

More importantly I soon realized that the encouragement principle applied to every aspect of our relationship. The way a person feels really affects the way they perform. Kit and I have since taught many marriage seminars. I frequently ask husbands, "Do you want a better wife? You'll have one if you learn to encourage and build up the one you already have." Husbands, likewise, can improve through sincere and godly encouragement from their wives.

Although my lesson began with Kit playing tennis, God used it to make me into an encouraging person. Kit and I later served as missionaries for 19 years. We spoke and trained leaders in 37 countries outside of America. God developed in me the ability to encourage leaders, which ultimately led to ongoing ministries around the world. Even in our current retirement, Kit and I continue as volunteers traveling to equip and encourage missionary leaders. I'm grateful that God used tennis to build into me a biblical principle that has enriched so many lives, starting with ours.

# PERSONAL *commitment*

Everyone said I was a good kid. I made good grades, went to Sunday School, and said "Yes, Sir" and "No, Ma'am" to my elders. I went away to college, and things were about the same. I was on the Dean's List and had a car, a job, and a girlfriend. Everyone said I had it made. But inside I knew differently. For one thing, I lay awake at night wondering what would happen to me when I died. Also, I had a terrible temper and would throw and break items when events didn't go my way. Worst of all, I had a tendency to use people to get what I wanted. As a result, I didn't have any real friends, only acquaintances.

    A guy I had gone to high school with invited me to attend a Bible study. The study focused on "How to know you are a Christian." One scripture particularly interested me: "And the testimony is this, that God has given us eternal life, and this life is in His Son. He who has the Son has the life; he who does not have the Son of God does not have the life. These things I have written to you who believe in the name of the Son of God, so that you may know that you have eternal life." (1 John 5:11–13)

Previously, I had a vague idea that God had a balance scale in heaven. He would put the good things you had done on one side and the bad things you had done on the other side. The scale would determine the way you would go. But you couldn't know which way that would be until you died.

Then I started to ask a lot of questions. I asked, "Where did Cain get his wife?" and "How did Noah get all the animals on the ark?" I never got all those answers, but I became convinced by the character of the Bible study leaders that Jesus Christ is real and that He could change my life.

One night, in the privacy of my dorm room, I prayed a prayer something like this: "Lord Jesus, I know I have sinned against You. Thank You for dying on the cross for my sins. Please come into my life to be my Lord and Savior. Make me the kind of person You want me to be." And immediately I felt . . . nothing. I didn't feel any different. But I knew that Jesus would keep His promise and had come into my life.

Very soon, my life started to change. First, I didn't have to worry about what would happen to me when I died. Then I learned to trust Him in many situations, and my temper improved. Then God taught me how to really care for other people, and soon I had the kind of friends I'd always wanted. And the best friend He gave me is my wife, Kit.

I'm still a long way from being Mr. Perfect. But I know that everything I have, everything I am, and everything I ever will be, I owe to what my Lord Jesus Christ has done for me.

# What is a more than ordinary life?

Each person's life is unique and special. In that sense, there is no such thing as an ordinary life. However, many people yearn for lives more special: excitement, adventure, romance, purpose, character. Our site is dedicated to the premise that any life can be more than ordinary.

At **MoreThanOrdinaryLives.com** you will find:

- inspiring stories
- entertaining novels
- ideas and resources
- free downloads

https://morethanordinarylives.com/

# Challenge Series

## by Kit and Drew Coons

### Challenge for Two
### Book One

A series of difficult circumstances have forced Dave and Katie Parker into early retirement. Searching for new life and purpose, the Parkers take a wintertime job house sitting an old Victorian mansion. The picturesque river town in southeastern Minnesota is far from the climate and culture of their home near the Alabama Gulf Coast.

But dark secrets sleep in the mansion. A criminal network has ruthlessly intimidated the community since the timber baron era of the 19th century. Residents have been conditioned to look the other way.

The Parkers' questions about local history and clues they discover in the mansion bring an evil past to light and create division in the small community. While some fear the consequences of digging up the truth, others want freedom from crime and justice for victims. Faced with personal threats, the Parkers must decide how to respond for themselves and for the good of the community.

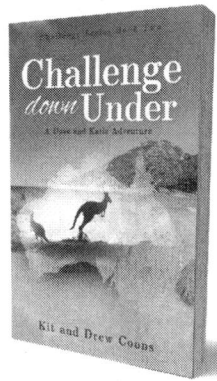

### Challenge Down Under
**Book Two**

———————

Dave and Katie Parker's only son, Jeremy, is getting married in Australia. In spite of initial reservations, the Parkers discover that Denyse is perfect for Jeremy and that she's the daughter they've always wanted. But she brings with her a colorful and largely dysfunctional Aussie family. Again Dave and Katie are fish out of water as they try to relate to a boisterous clan in a culture very different from their home in South Alabama.

After the wedding, Denyse feels heartbroken that her younger brother, Trevor, did not attend. Details emerge that lead Denyse to believe her brother may be in trouble. Impressed by his parents' sleuthing experience in Minnesota, Jeremy volunteers them to locate Trevor. Their search leads them on an adventure through Australia and New Zealand.

Unfortunately, others are also searching for Trevor, with far more sinister intentions. With a talent for irresponsible chicanery inherited from his family, Trevor has left a trail of trouble in his wake and has been forced into servitude. Can Dave and Katie locate him in time?

### Challenge in Mobile
### Book Three

Dave and Katie Parker regret that their only child Jeremy, his wife Denyse, and their infant daughter live on the opposite side of the world. Unexpectedly, Jeremy calls to ask his father's help finding an accounting job in the US. Katie urges Dave to do whatever is necessary to find a job for Jeremy near Mobile. Dave's former accounting firm has floundered since his departure. The Parkers risk their financial security by purchasing full ownership of the struggling firm to make a place for Jeremy.

Denyse finds South Alabama fascinating compared to her native Australia. She quickly resumes her passion for teaching inner-city teenagers. Invited by Katie, other colorful guests arrive from Australia and Minnesota to experience Gulf Coast culture. Aided by their guests, Dave and Katie examine their faith after Katie receives discouraging news from her doctors.

Political, financial, and racial tensions have been building in Mobile. Bewildering financial expenditures of a client create suspicions of criminal activity. Denyse hears disturbing rumors from her students. A hurricane from the Gulf of Mexico exacerbates the community's tensions. Dave and Katie are pulled into a crisis that requires them to rise to a new level of more than ordinary.

# More from Kit and Drew Coons

### The Ambassadors

Two genetically engineered beings unexpectedly arrive on Earth. Unlike most extraterrestrials depicted in science fiction, the pair is attractive, personable, and telegenic–the perfect talk show guests. They have come to Earth as ambassadors bringing an offer of partnership in a confederation of civilizations. Technological advances are offered as part of the partnership. But humans must learn to cooperate among themselves to join.

Molly, a young reporter, and Paul, a NASA scientist, have each suffered personal tragedy and carry emotional baggage. They are asked to tutor the ambassadors in human ways and to guide them on a worldwide goodwill tour. Molly and Paul observe as the extraterrestrials commit faux pas while experiencing human culture. They struggle trying to define a romance and partnership while dealing with burdens of the past.

However, mankind finds implementing actual change difficult. Clashing value systems and conflicts among subgroups of humanity erupt. Inevitably, rather than face difficult choices, fearmongers in the media start to blame the messengers. Then an uncontrolled biological weapon previously created by a rogue country tips the world into chaos. Molly, Paul, and the others must face complex moral decisions about what being human means and the future of mankind.

# MINI SERIES

**More Than Ordinary Challenges—**
Dealing with the Unexpected

**More Than Ordinary Marriage—**
A Higher Level

**More Than Ordinary Faith—**
Why Does God Allow Suffering?

**More Than Ordinary Wisdom—**
Stories of Faith and Folly

**More Than Ordinary Abundance—**
From Kit's Heart

**More Than Ordinary Choices—**
Making Good Decisions

Visit **https://morethanordinarylives.com/**
for more information.

# About the Authors

Kit and Drew Coons met while Christian missionaries in Africa in 1980. As humorous speakers specializing in strengthening relationships, they have taught in every part of the US and in thirty-nine other countries. For two years, the Coonses lived and served in New Zealand and Australia. They are keen cultural observers and incorporate their many adventures into their writing. Kit and Drew are unique in that they speak and write as a team.

Made in the USA
San Bernardino, CA
24 September 2018